Samuel de Champlain

Discover The Life Of An Explorer

Trish Kline

Rourke Publishing LLC
Vero Beach, Florida 32964

PHOTO CREDITS:
©Archive Photos: cover, page 18; ©Canadian Heritage, National Archives of
Canada:title page, pages 7, 9, 21; ©Culver Pictures: page 10; ©James P.
Rowan; pages 12, 17; ©Artville LLC; page 13; ©Corbis Images: page 15; Library
of Congress: page 4

EDITORIAL SERVICES:
Pamela Schroeder

Library of Congress Cataloging-in-Publication Data

Kline, Trish.
      Samuel de Champlain / Trish Kline.
          p. cm. — (Discover the life of an explorer)
      Includes bibliographical references and index
      ISBN 1-58952-070-X
      1. Champlain, Samuel de, 1567-1635—Juvenile. 2.
Explorers—America—Biography—Juvenile literature. 3.
Explorers—France—Biography—Juvenile literature. 4. New
France—Discovery and exploration—French—Juvenile literature. 5.
America—Discovery and exploration—French—Juvenile literature.
[1. Champlain, Samuel de, 1567-1635. 2.Explorers. 3. American—
Discovery and exploration. 4. New France—Discovery and
exploration.] I. Title

      F1030.1 .K58 2001
      971.01'13'092—dc21
      B]   2001019372

TABLE OF CONTENTS

THE SON OF A SEA CAPTAIN

Samuel de Champlain was born in 1567. He lived in France. His father was a sea captain. As a boy, Champlain learned about the sea. As a young man, he became a soldier. In 1599, Samuel de Champlain became the captain of a ship. He spent two years sailing around the West Indies and Mexico. On these **voyages**, Champlain learned how to **navigate** ships. He learned **geography** and how to make maps.

Champlain was a soldier and a ship captain.

FIRST VOYAGE

In 1603 Champlain made his first voyage to North America. He explored the St. Lawrence River near the present-day city of Montreal, Canada. He chose a place to build a fur trading company. He made friends with local Native Americans. The Native Americans traded furs for cloth and metal wares such as knives.

Champlain made a map of the area. It showed a large bay to the north and water to the west. These bodies of water were named Hudson Bay and the Great Lakes.

Champlain trades with Native Americans.

A COLD WINTER

In 1604 Champlain made a second voyage to North America. He explored the Atlantic Coast. He was looking for a good place to start a **colony**. He chose a spot on an island near the St. Croix River. Soon settlers moved there.

Champlain and his men search for a place to start a colony.

The winter was very cold. Half of the 79 settlers died. Champlain **survived**. He stayed at the colony for three years. He explored more of the area and made maps. These maps showed the Atlantic Coast.

Native Americans helped Champlain explore the area around the colony.

Champlain found and mapped Lake Ontario.

Champlain explored the area around the Great Lakes.

A NEW SETTLEMENT

In 1608 Champlain started another colony. Many of the settlers died from **scurvy**. The few that survived stayed in the colony. This was the first colony in Canada. Today this colony is known as the city of Quebec.

Quebec was the first French colony in Canada.

GREAT LAKES AND RIVERS

In 1611 Champlain built a trading post at Mont Royal. He was named general of New France. Champlain spent time exploring the area. He found many rivers and lakes. He drew these bodies of water on his maps. Today we call these areas the Ottawa River, Lake Ontario, and Lake Champlain.

Lake Champlain bears the name of the French explorer.

KARST

CAPTURED!

In 1629 New France was at war with England. The settlement of Quebec was captured by English soldiers. Champlain was taken prisoner. He was sent to a prison in England. After the war, New France was returned to French rule. In 1633 Champlain was set free. He returned to Quebec. He lived there until his death in 1635. He was 68 years old.

The English held Champlain prisoner for 4 years.

THE FATHER OF NEW FRANCE

Champlain was an **explorer** and sea captain. He was also a map maker, writer, and leader. He helped begin many colonies in the young country of New France. Soon New France was given the name Canada. Champlain drew the maps that helped new settlers come to Canada.

Samuel de Champlain is often called the "Father of New France."

An early French map showing the St. Lawrence River and the Atlantic Coast

de Tormenta

de Golfan

Baya dus Medaus

Golfo de Merolro

gue nai.

Azabub

S. Maria.
C. de Marz

Terra Cortereale.

Bacallaos.

NOVA FRANCIA ET CANADA 1597.

CANADA

Terra doulce de chiraye

Le Sept Ales
Banc de S. Iacques

Costa du nost

S. Laurens
S. Nicolas
C. Tienet
Postillon
Acaris isles
Brest
P. de Iacques Cartier
Blanc Sablon
C. Belle Isle

Honguedo

de Dom

Y. de Assumptione
Sinus S. Laurenty.

Auque
Thecondaly
Catiel
Hosul la rocte
Gonea
Statan fto.
Igne chorayne

Estrout de S. Pierre
Cap. de Monmorency
Cap. de S. Aloise

NOVA FRAN
CIA.

Hochlga

Primer salt
Y. Donpllans
Le Prepalongo.
La Fait.
Y. de Coslli.

S. Martin

Golfo de chaleur
Baye de chaleur

Laguille
Chambriant
Hommorancy
Y. dorleans alys de Baccho.

Y. les ligres
Cap. de mibe
Rospelay

C. desperansa

B. S. Lunaire

ilaga.

Ilaga flu.

R. de lungres
C. S. Iacti alys Portlants
Cap. de S. Ioan
S. Pauli
C. Real
Cortiereo
R. Pincoro
C. Doeme
C. de Breton
Brize

IMPORTANT DATES TO REMEMBER

1567	Born in France.
1599	Became captain of a ship and sailed around the West Indies and Mexico.
1603	First voyage to North America. Explored the St. Lawrence River near Canada.
1604	Second voyage to North America. Mapped the Atlantic Coast.
1608	Started a colony in present-day Quebec, Canada.
1611	Built a trading post at Mont Royal.
1629	Taken prisoner by the English.
1633	Released from prison. Returned to Quebec.
1635	Died in Quebec, Canada.

GLOSSARY

colony (KAHL eh nee) — a place in a country where people live but are ruled by another country

explorer (ik SPLOR er) — someone who travels to unknown places

geography (jee AHG re fee) — the study of the Earth and of its plant and animal life

navigate (NAV i gayt) — to steer the way you want to go

scurvy (SKUR vee) — disease caused by poor diet

survived (ser VYVD) — stayed alive

voyages (VOY ij ez) — trips to far away places

INDEX

Further Reading

Jacobs, William Jay. *Champlain: A Life of Courage.* Franklin Watts, 1994.
O'Brien, Patrick. *Samuel de Champlain*. Raintree Steck-Vaughn, 2000.

Websites To Visit

www.encarta.msn.com
www.blupete.com
www.gale.com

About The Author

Trish Kline is a seasoned curriculum writer. She has written a great number of nonfiction books for the school and library market. Her print publishing credits include two dozen books as well as hundreds of newspaper and magazine articles, anthologies, short stories, poetry, and plays. She currently resides in Helena, Montana.

jB
CHAMPLAI
N

Kline, Trish.

Samuel de Champlain.

$18.60

DATE			